AMARANTH

BY EDWIN ARLINGTON ROBINSON

COLLECTED POEMS
  Avon's Harvest
  Captain Craig
  Cavender's House
  The Children of the Night
  Dionysus in Doubt
  Lancelot
  Merlin
  Tristram
  The Man Against the Sky
  The Man Who Died Twice
  The Three Taverns
  The Town Down the River

CAVENDER'S HOUSE

ROMAN BARTHOLOW

SONNETS 1889–1927

THE GLORY OF THE NIGHTINGALES

THE THREE TAVERNS

TRISTRAM

MATTHIAS AT THE DOOR

NICODEMUS

TALIFER

AMARANTH

AMARANTH

By Edwin Arlington Robinson

NEW YORK

The Macmillan Company

1934

TO THE MEMORY OF
H. DEAN ROBINSON

AMARANTH

AMARANTH

I

After a sleep and an awakening
That only freedom earned of servitude
And error may deserve, Fargo saw first,
As always now, before him on the wall,
The one of all his pictures he had spared
When wisdom, lashing heart-sick heroism
To mortal zeal, would let him spare no more.
They were all gone now, and the last faint ghost
Of an unreal regret had followed them.
A voice like one of an undying friend
Whom he had always known and never seen
Had pierced and wounded him till he was warned
Of only one escape; and he was free.
An oily-fiery sacrifice one day,
With nature smiling at him as if pleased,
Had left him contemplating gratefully
A wealth of smoke and ashes. He had heard
The voice until its calm reiterations
Were no more to be stifled with denial,
Or longer to be borne; and he was free.
There were ten years between him and those
    ashes

That were behind him now to make him young.
At thirty-five he had been cleansed and cured;
At forty-five he could look back and laugh—
Or sigh, if need be. With a sleepy glance
At his accusing remnant on the wall,
He rubbed his eyes, and thought. It was not bad;
It was about as good as a few thousand
That hands no worse than his would do some-
    where
Before the day was over. Sunday morning
Would never stay those hands. Art has no rest
Until, unlike the old guard, it surrenders,
Or, like the old guard, dies. He had surren-
    dered,
So not to greet himself among the slain
Before he should be dead. He was alive,
And had no longer a dim will to die,
Or to get up. No bells of destiny
Frightened or vexed him with recrimination,
Or with remorse; no trumpet of loud reason
Told why he should not cherish and encourage
An unforbidden willingness to sleep.

Now there was nothing that a world awake
Would have called light, or darkness. Where he
    stood
He could see wharves and ships that he had
    seen
Somewhere before, where there were lights and
    sounds

And stars, and the cold wash of a slow tide
So far below him that he had not looked
Too long to see it there. All this had been
Before, but never a silence like this now
On ships and wharves and water could have
    been
Since moving time began. He had come back
Once more to a lost world where all was gone
But ghostly shapes that had no life in them,
And to the wrong world he would once have left
By the wrong door. The old door was now open,
And he had merely to gaze down again
To know the darkness of its invitation,
There in that evil water. Without sound
Or motion, there it was. There was no sun
Or moon to make him wonder whether day
Or night revealed it, and there were no stars;
And that forbidding water was not the same
That once had called him. It was calling now;
And all the silences, stiller than time
Between the stars, if anywhere there were stars,
Were calling. The awakening and escape
For which he had thanked God, the sacrifice
For which God had apparently thanked him,
The world that he was born for and had found
Before it was past having, all were gone,
And were remembered shadows. It was here
That he had been before there was a voice
To stop him and to ask him if the cross
He carried was the cross that fitted him.

[3]

A cross, like many another misfit burden,
May be thrown off—sometimes, the voice had
    said;
Throw it, and you are free. He had been free
Only in fancy. He was here again
By the same water that was not the same
As one that once had waited to receive him.

He made a slow step forward and looked down
Despairingly at a black flood of silence
That had no ripple of life. The world was dead
That held him; and so far as he could fathom
The depth and end of its past vanities,
No clearer way was anywhere left for him
Than a swift one to darkness down before him,
And waiting for him. If he had for years
Carried a cross that was not his to carry,
Believing it was art, and had been dreaming
Of years when it was done with and behind him,
Why should he wait? If he had only dreamed
Of a transformed and sound accomplishment,
Imaginably the sounder for delay,
Why should he pause or faintly temporize
Where there was nothing left? He gazed again
Below him, and the water was still there.

And there was more than water. Near behind
    him,
He could hear steps, and slowly a low voice:
"You heard me once, and once you heeded me;

And in my words you found deliverance.
I did not ask you then to look at me,
But you may see me now. I have come down
To tell you that I cannot let you sink
So quickly and so easily from my sight.
I have come down here to the end of things
To find you, as I found you here before—
Before you heard my voice. Why are you here,
When you must know so darkly where you are?
Why, friend, have you come back to the wrong
    world?"

He listened, without power or will to turn,
And only by enforcement hazarded
The sight of what was there. Had this been life
That he was living, and had this been earth
Where he was standing, he would have been
    shaken
No more than by the voice of any stranger
Saying strange things. But as he heard, he knew
That whatsoever presence there might be
Behind him, there was more there than a man;
And though no more a coward than another,
He knew that fear had found his heart. He knew
Also that he must turn, that he must know.
Too much that was mysterious had already
Amazed him and oppressed him. He must know
More of this place that was a place of death,
And more of what was in it still alive,
And with a tongue to speak. He made himself

Turn round, and saw why he was not alone.
If it was man, it might have been all men
And women there as one. All who have been,
And all alive and all unborn were there
Before him, and their eyes were watching him
Out of those two that might have been the eyes
Of death, if death were life. He looked at them,
But only as a fool looks at the sun,
And for about as long. More fire was in them
Than he could meet, though he felt glimmerings,
And shadows that were less than memories,
Of having met them once and welcomed them
Incredibly, and their appointed purpose.
If that was true, they could not then have been
So flaming or so fierce. Meanwhile the face
That held them, and held him, was more the face
Of man than of his maker; and the more
He looked at it, the less was it the face
Of one unknown. If it was man before him,
Not even a presence so unnamable
Was unapproachable. If it had no name,
And still had speech, it might say things to him
That he had better know.

                         "You meditate
Only the truth, for you had better know,"
It said; and a sad shadow of a smile
Said too much more: "So you will follow me,
And leave this willing water far behind you.
You sought it once, and would have none of it,

When you had heard my voice. For I was here
To see, my friend, as you were here to listen.
You heard; and then there was no need to see
    me—
Not then. But since you have come back to me,
To the wrong world whence I delivered you,
Now you shall see. For those who damn them-
    selves
By coming back, voices are not enough.
They must have ears and eyes to know for certain
Where they have come, and to what punishment.
Only the reconciled or the unwakened
Have resignation or ambition here;
And I have here no power that I call mine;
The power is more than mine."

                   "If that be so,"
Said Fargo, "and if you are not the Devil,
What means are yours to make me follow you?"
He trembled as he said it, and half feared
The blast of a divine annihilation
As a last answer. But a sadder smile,
Betraying an approval that was useless,
Followed instead, and silence. "Why do you
    care
Whether I go with you, or go the way
That I came here to take? What matters it
To you, whatever you are, which way I go?
I thought once I was free, and far from here.
I dreamed all that."

[7]

"Freedom is mostly dreams,
My friend. As for your coming and your going,
I should not care—if it were not my doom
To save, and when discredited or feared,
To quench or to destroy. I do not say
That for some exigencies of my office
I am less grieved than I am gratified,
Or that I am more loved than I am hated.
Only, I say that you will follow me
Because no other road is left for you;
For the same law that holds the stars apart
Holds you and me together. Come with me,
And you will come to nothing wholly strange.
I wish you might not come. But since you
        must,
We may as well progress. It is not far
From here, and you are not afraid of graves;
For we are in a land where there are many,
And many to be made. Shall we go now?"

Resentment, recognized and disavowed
As a futility not worth fighting for,
Made Fargo plead for parley—as one will,
Even when he knows: "Before I follow you
May I pray, briefly, for the privilege
Of asking what you are? Are you a man,
Or are you spirit? If you are a man,
There is a name for you. I'm never at ease
When a man tells me I shall follow him,
And has no name."

[8]

The stranger's face betrayed
A weariness: "But you would follow him,
Perforce and of a surety. Man or spirit,
He has a name. The name is Amaranth—
The flower that never fades. Where we are go-
        ing
You may hear more of it; and among the graves
Around you now, my friend, nothing insists
On pleasantry. For those who are down in them
Went mostly with no smile. Some looked at me
And cursed me, and then died. Some looked and
        live,
And are indifferent. They are the reconciled,
Who neither live nor die. Now you may see
Before you the gay Tavern of the Vanquished,
Which has been here so long that no man says
Who carried the first stone."

                        More with a feel
Of having flown or floated, with no motion,
Than of remembered steps that he had made,
Fargo surveyed a place illuminated
By the same changeless light that had revealed
Still wharves and water and fear-laden ships
That had no life on board, and was not light
That shines on earth. It was a place so old
That all who entered it remembered it.
Dark walls and darker shadows, and dark rafters,
Looked always to have been there; and old
        floors,

[9]

Hewn of a wood that was unwearable,
Might never have been trees. Tables and chairs
Of an unspoilable antiquity
Were dim with centuries of welcomings
And shadowed with farewells; and with no end
That was to see, the long place was alive
With nothing that was any longer there.

"Where have I seen all this before, I wonder,"
Said Fargo to himself; and Amaranth,
Appearing, answered: "There are times and
    scenes
Which for so long have been the life of you
That they are melted in the veiling mist
Of years behind you. You were here before,
But you had then your zeal and ignorance
Between you and your vision of it now.
Since you are here to stay, you will see more:
You will see memories that you may have felt,
And ecstasies that are not memories yet;
And you will ask of me in vain to tell you
Why the rest cannot see. Some of them will;
And some of them, caring no more to live
Without the calm of their concealed misgivings,
Will die; while others who care more for life
Without a spur than for no life at all,
Will somehow live. I do not ask of any
To meet the mirrors that are in my eyes;
But if they must, they will. You see the place
Is filled now, and you mourn to see so many

[10]

In the wrong world—some young and unsub-
    dued,
Some older and untold, some very old,
And mercifully not to be disturbed
Or undeceived. And why must you be here?
After my saving you, so long ago,
There by that water where you were today,
Why, why, must you come back?"

                Before he sought
The first word of an answer, a lean stranger
Called him. And in a moment, without walking,
He made himself informally a guest
At a round table, where they welcomed him,
And found without confusion or commotion
A place for him, although there was none
    there.
"Because we saw you," the lean stranger said,
"With Amaranth, and because we know him better
Than you, if the Lord cares, will ever know him,
I beckoned you. Beware of Amaranth;
For if you look too long into his eyes,
And see what's there to find, you will see more
Than a good God, if not preoccupied,
Would let be known to the least diligent
Of his misguided and ambitious worms.
I am one Evensong, a resident
For life in the wrong world, where I made
    music,
And make it still. It is not necessary,

But habit that has outlived revelation
May pipe on to the end. Listen to this: "

The stranger suddenly produced a flute,
And played while his companions heard and
     smiled
Resignedly as at a story told
Long since to death. "A theme for a quintette,"
Said Evensong. "It sounds like nothing now,
But once it sounded as if God had made it.
Therefore I say, beware of Amaranth,
If you are not the mightier. You are not,
Or you would not be here. Your name is
     Fargo—
Which is a good name, and has overtones.
Permit me to present the rest of us:
This disillusioned fellow-citizen,
Whose coat needs ink and scissors where it frays,
Is Edward Figg, whose eyes, like yours and
     mine,
See backwards. There is more in him to worship
Than has come out. He would not strangle you;
He would not steal your money, or your wife;
But he saw wrong, and is a good man wasted.
Once, in a cruel trance of aberration,
He thought himself enamored of the law—
The last of all employment possible
For one of his construction.—Our next friend,
Who sees also behind him, will assuage
Your qualms and aches that are not memories,

Or of the spirit. He is Doctor Styx,
Who might, perhaps, God knows, have been a
    diver,
A silversmith, or a ventriloquist,
But not, as you behold, what playful fate
Misled him to attempt. Error prevailed,
And here he is. The springs of interest
Are broken in him, and you hear him creak.
Yet lesser men than he, in the right world,
Are crowned for staying there.—You see beside
    him
A worthy friend who has a crying conscience
Because he knew before he was informed.
The Reverend Pascal Flax, from all we learn
Of his decline, became a clergyman
Because he liked to talk, and to be seen
As one anointed for an elevation.
But he saw nothing that he could believe,
And one day said no more. He left his flock
To a new shepherd, and you see him now—
A man of rust, and of a covered worth
Never to shine again since Amaranth
Withered him with his eye. But he still talks,
Unless he drinks too long, and younger men
Who smile, and do not yet know where they
    are,
Will buy his knowledge with a condescension
That one day will be sorrow. Two of them
Are with us here, and they are not so young
Now as they were at thirty. The slight one

Who sits erect, impervious, and secure,
Is Pink the poet. He cuts and sets his words
With an exotic skill so scintillating
That no two proselytes who worship them
Are mystified in the same way exactly.
All who believe themselves at one with him
Will have a private and a personal Pink,
And their unshared interpretation of him—
Which makes him universal for the few,
And may be all he wants.—Now there re-
    mains
One more of us. This giant with a beard
Blacker than paint, and with his red shirt open
To show us what it is to have a throat,
Is Atlas, who was a king stevedore
Before he was a painter. Now he paints
Because he must; which is, it seems, the reason
Why there are painters, poets, or musicians,
And why so many of them come here to drink,
If you see what I mean. You are a painter,
And must have eyes. Whatever you see with
    them,
Don't pity us, for you are one of us—
Unless he lets you go. Once in a while
Not even the eyes of Amaranth will hold
A victim to his doom, but that's not always;
For the most part we stay. As you may guess,
Barring our well-illusioned visitors,
Who still enjoy the comfort of their scorn,
We have encountered Amaranth face to face,

And eye to eye; and as we are, you see us.
We are the reconciled initiates,
Who know that we are nothing in men's eyes
That we set out to be—and should have been,
Had we seen better. We see better now."

"You do not see so well," the poet said,
"That you are not all burrowing in a past,
Where there is mostly darkness and dead roots
That you believe are juicy. If you like them,
Eat them until you choke."

                        "Dear, dear," said Flax,
"Why such a violence? If the roots are dead,
Why for so many stormy centuries
Have the trees lived? If you are tired of them,
Young man, you might resolve to have them
    down.
We shall not fail, we old ones, to be present."

"I am not young," Pink said: "I am as old
As art; and where death has a life in it,
I can see living death. If you don't see it,
You old ones are the children, who have nothing
To play with but a few poor dusty toys
Left in a garret by your grandfathers.
And when you're tired of them, you have your
    roots.
Good God, I'm sick of roots."

"I fear, young man,"
Said Doctor Styx, "that you are sick of more
Than roots. There are misgivings eating you,
Like borers in a tree—and in its roots."

"And you had best remember," said the lawyer,
"That we are more acquainted with misgivings,
And more resigned to them, than you are yet.
Ours have all hatched, and are consuming us
Inside, young man. We set ourselves to grow
In the wrong earth, and soon we had no roots.
If there's no shade beneath our foliage,
There's evidence to say why."

"I shall exist
Without the tonic of your sad example,"
The poet said. "And not so much 'young man.'
If you four are the foliage and the fruit
Of your world, I have longings for another;
And so, if there's a foresight in his frenzy,
Has comrade Atlas."

"I don't know," growled Atlas,
"What you are saying. And if Pink cares, let him.
I'm sorry to agree with him, but once
I'll have to. There are too damned many roots.
I don't know poetry, but I do know paint;
And if you'll spare me, I'll go back to it.
You don't need me—for I was here to drink,

And hear the Reverend talk. But he's not talk-
    ing
Today; and I don't talk unless you tell me
Things about paint that you don't know about."
He coughed, and with a massive confidence
That had no falterings, he lounged away.

"You may be safer if you follow Atlas,"
Amaranth said to Pink: "I came in time
To hear you, but your vehemence obscured me.
In art you must esteem yourselves or perish,
Which is not saying that esteem is genius,
Or violence independence. I have still—
And I am older than the youngest poet
Who has no more to learn—to recognize
And worship, as a man more than divine,
One who is independent. I am not,
Or I should not be here. If I had will
To make me wings, and power to fly with them
So far away from this insidious place
That all here might forget me, none of you
Should have to quail again at my approach,
Or fear to meet the mirrors in my eyes.
For most, there is more joy, if not more wis-
    dom,
In seeing not too well."

                "Who fears—or quails?"
Pink asked of Ámaranth, who closed his eyes,
And with a weary smile of helplessness

[17]

Opened them slowly: "Do you think, young
    man,
That you, of all the many who have hoarded
Strength to say that, will prove yourself elected
Never to quail? Now I should avoid quailing
To my last hour of arrogance on earth;
I should not rush to see myself too well,
Or to behold myself too finally,
If I were you. Dreams have a kindly way,
Sometimes, if they are not explored or shaken,
Of lasting glamorously. Many have lasted
All a man's life, sparing him, to the grave,
His value and his magnitude. In this
One sees, or feels, if so attuned and tempered,
An ordered prudence, or an adumbration
Of more than we arrange. If I were you,
I should not wrench or scorch myself unduly.
Why not let these injurious agitations
Go pleasantly to rest and be forgotten?"

Pink rose, and trembled: "For you, Amaranth,
I do not know you, and I do not like you.
And you would not be missed if you should
    shrink
And fade for ever."

       "The flower that never fades
Will not do that, young man," said Evensong:
"You cannot scare him, and you cannot kill him.
Four of us here have seen him eye to eye,

And we are still alive. We are not kings,
But still we live. You are afraid of him,
And you had better stay so. There's no shame
In wisdom; and there's often, if we knew it,
A deal of healthful and grief-saving fear."

"Damn it, I was not asking you," said Pink,
"For your assistance or commiseration.
When I shall see no longer where I'm going,
I shall not ask the dead."

                            "I drink reproof,"
Said Evensong: "My frailty copes in vain
With fevered youth. If your new flowers and
    trees
Require no roots, why vex and scald the soil
With so much acid? May not the new truth
    sleep
In a new bed, and still be comfortable?"

Pink smote him with a scowl, and then he said,
To Amaranth, "All this may end as well
At once as ever. I have seen your face,
And have not shivered at the sight of it,
Or not inordinately. If you fancy
That I'm afflicted with a fear to meet
Myself, and what I am and am to be,
I'm at your service. Let me see what's hidden—
And now; and let me learn how far my sight
Outsees the truth. If your friends here have
    seen

The face of God—your pardon, my mistake—
And still sit here alive, if not renowned,
I fear no shrinkage."

              "You will have it so,"
Said Amaranth. "Come here, then. Look at me;
Look in my eyes. . . . Now tell me what you
    see,
And whether you should pay for staying here
Your price of dust. Is it a lawful price?
I should say not, but I am not the Law
That says what men shall do—though I may
    wish,
Too late, that you had gone when Atlas went."

The poet held his hands against his eyes,
And for a while stood rigid. Then he spoke:
"Forgive me; this is more surprise than terror,"
He said to Fargo: "But it rankles always
To share a disadvantage with a stranger.
You need not look at me, or look away.
The rest of you may look, for all I care,
Back to yourselves as you believed you were,
And then regard yourselves as you are now.
I wish you a long life in the wrong world,
Where you seem well-adjusted and at ease.
I shall go on as well without your comment
As I have lived without your comprehension.
Amaranth has no reason for remorse,
Or self-reproach. I asked, and I received.

The bowl is broken, and I'm not afraid.
Excuse me, while I go and hang myself."

"He will hang hard, I fear," said Doctor Styx,
Who watched him as he walked away, erect
And unsuspected by the multitude,
Who drank and sang and saw him only as one
Among so many. "Poets are of a toughness,
And they are slow to kill," the doctor said
To Fargo: "Shall we drink to his departure?"

"Before we do," said Evensong, "permit me
To play for him the burden of a dirge—
An elegy, as it were—which I prepared,
Anticipating an event like this.
It is not long, and it is not immortal;
It is not overwhelming, or supreme.
Listen to this." He played, and they all smiled
As at another story told too often.
"You don't extol it, or not noisily;
No more do I. Now let us drink to Pink,
And may our new companion Fargo join us.
He's not yet reconciled, and has the manner
Of one unwilling to be one of us.
Time will attend to that; for he is here,
The Lord knows why, and has been here before;
And here he must remain—which is a pity.
So then, to Pink—and to an easy voyage
Over a lonely sea that shall be ours
In turn to cross. If when our voyage begins

There may not be much weeping on the wharves,
We shall not care; and those we leave behind
Will suffer less than if they needed us."

"There's more percipience in you, Evensong,
Than there is music," said the doctor, rising;
And they all stood erect, with a precision
That was abrupt and ceremonial,
And soldierly: "Since our young friend has
    paused
And faltered on the wrong road to Damascus,
Having seen too much light, we'll drink to him,
And to ourselves, and to our new friend Fargo.
Let our new friend regard us, and see twice
The end, before he says he is our brother;
For we are here by ways not on the chart
Of time that we read once as ours to follow.
Time here is all today and yesterday,
For in the wrong world there is no tomorrow.
We stayed and lingered, only to be lost
In twilight while we saw where we were going;
We slept and rested, and we slept again,
Till we awoke where there was no returning.
So let us drink to all we should have been,
Telling ourselves again it is no matter;
The more we lie, the more must we believe.
Similia similibus curantur."

II

Now there were streets and houses. There was
    nothing
But empty streets, and houses that were still.
There was a tavern far away somewhere
Behind him, but without a guide or sign
To lead him, there was no way back to it.
He could remember what had happened there,
But now he was outside, and was alone.
A door that was forgotten must have opened,
And must have shut itself irrevocably
Against him; and all that was long ago.
He was alone again. By the same light
That was not light, in which he had seen first
Those wharves of silence, and the silent ships,
Now there were only unfamiliar streets,
And houses that were strange. If there were
    men
And women hidden in them, they were silent;
And if they were aware of a man walking,
Lost and alone, they were not occupied
With his identity, or with his presence
Or destination. Fargo, had they asked him,

Could not have said to them where he was
    going,
For he was going nowhere. He knew that;
And with a certitude that was abysmal,
And in a manner fearsome, he walked on,
Hearing his aimless footfall on the pavement,
And hearing nothing else—till all at once,
And round a corner that was imminent,
Came suddenly the sound of other feet,
Heavy and hard, and of harsh laughter mixed
With words not good to hear. Surprise and rage
Assailed him at the sound of his own name,
Spoken with ribald and unwholesome scorn
By one that with a mouth and with a mind
That was unclean foretold ambiguously
Disaster and extinction.

                  Fargo stopped
As if a wall of glass had hindered him
Invisibly from going farther forward,
And waited, more in anger than in fear,
For what might be approaching. No long time
Was gone before he saw surrounding him
Their soiled and uncouth shapes, and their lewd
    faces
Watching him with a glee that had no mercy;
And he saw picks and shovels on their shoulders
Before he saw their eyes; and he saw clay
Upon their feet before he heard his name
Spoken again.

"So Fargo has come back,"
Said one of them. Had each not been as foul
As all the rest, he might have been the foulest,
And so a sort of captain, Fargo thought,
Or noisome foreman. "Yes, he has come back,"
Said a voice farther off. And then the first:
"Yes, Fargo has come back to the wrong world.
He left us, but he loves the sight of us,
And cannot die without us. Shall we tell him
How long he has to live, and how far down
We bury them, who come back? There is a
 place
That's waiting for you, Fargo. Come with us,
And see what happens when a man comes back.
It's a good place to see—if you are blind;
And most are blind who go there."

        Fargo felt
His arms held bestially by noxious fingers;
And weaker for the fury that was in him,
Found himself pulled and pushed and dragged
 along,
His opposition only cursed and laughed at,
And all persuasion vain.

      "No more of that,"
Came then as a command; and Amaranth
Appeared as God might among torturers.
"You ghouls and scavengers that would possess
The dead before they die, scuttle and hide,

[25]

And wash your skins; or the next graves you
    make
Will be for you your beds."

                With a low snarl
That said surrender and obedience,
They faded and were gone, as if the wrath
Of Amaranth had made a vapor of them.
"What are you doing with the grave-diggers?"
He questioned; and he came as near as ever
He came to smiling: "Why resolve so early
On dissolution? Why have you forsaken
The good companionship that I prepared
For you there in the Tavern? If you saw them
Only as derelicts and castaways
Unworthy of your larger contemplation,
I shall not urge you now to contemplate
Your picture in my eyes. There will be time
For pictures more detached and recreative
Than yours may be, and with more drama in
    them.
Whether you see me as your friend or not,
You will be happier not too far from me,
And wiser for no ranging. To be lost
In the wrong world is twice to be astray,
For you are lost already. Come with me,
My friend; for you are shaken and amazed,
And are still fearful of the grave-diggers.
So come with me. You are not theirs—not
    yet."

Now there were stairs. "Be careful," Amaranth
     said,
"For some of them are gone. This house is old—
So old that many tenants have as children
Ascended here in sport, and are still here
As children. If you must be one of them,
Acommodation that will be sufficient
May soon be made for you. Out of this house
There's always going; and those who go, go far.
There are physicians here who cannot hold them,
Or cure themselves of an incessant wound
That now no retrospect of their tuition
In a wrong school shall heal; there are divines
Who long ago lost their divinity,
And are still feeling for a solid station;
There are philosophers who delve and starve
To say again what others have said better;
There are wan moralists and economists
Who write with screaming blood to save a world
That will not read them and will not be saved;
There are lost lawyers who have never pondered
Until too late, the law that was their sentence
To serve where they were never born to serve;
There are deceived inventors who still grope
For bridges that were never built for them
Between their dreams and their discrepancies;
There are spine-weary gardeners who are foiled
Because their fruits and flowers are not their
     friends;
And with all these there are as many others

As there are lives that are not to be lived—
Not here—but should have been, or many of
    them,
And well enough, had they been lived elsewhere.
Oh, this is an old house; and all the streets
You found and wandered in, and with no guide,
Are walled with houses that are populous
With tenants who have never found a home.
You have come back, my brother, to a city
Where there is nothing firm and nothing right.
Have you come back to it because you love it?
Was it for nothing that I set you free?"

"I see no answer shining in the dark,"
Said Fargo. "All I know is, I am here.
I have no other knowledge than a dimness
That is not quite remembrance, yet remembers.
I am not here because I would be here;
And God knows why I must."

                              Now there were doors.
At one of them, half open, Amaranth,
After a pause that might have been a warning
Or a command, led Fargo silently,
And with a downward eye, into a room
Where there was Evensong, Atlas the painter,
The Reverend Pascal Flax and Lawyer Figg,
And Doctor Styx—all gazing curiously,
And without anguish or astonishment,
At Pink the poet, who was hanging straight

And silent from a rafter. The dim wall
Behind him was more like a painted silence
Than like a wall; and the man hanging there
Was more a picture than he was a man
To his examiners.

        "Well, here we are,"
Said Evensong, who had produced his flute,
"And we may do no less for our late friend,
Whose love of us may not have been alone
The leavening of his unsustaining loaf,
Than play again the burden of my dirge—
My elegy, as it were—for his departure.
I pray for the collusion of your silence,
Which I'll interpret fondly as your patience.
I thank you gratefully. Pink, listen to this.
It's not ineffable, it's not absolute,
But it's at least a balm of harmlessness
For me in my defeat. So, Pink, be kind—
If so you may."

        While Evensong had blown
Reluctantly his funerary last,
The poet's eyes had slowly partly opened
And now his lips had moved: "If, Evensong,
I am worth only that for having lived,
I should have hastened and come earlier
To my condition here. If Amaranth
Had been less merciful, or indifferent,
He might have served as a more useful spirit

In forcing me to know. And here is Atlas,
Grinning at me because I told him once
What a crude opulence of mortality
There was in what he did. Did I not so,
Atlas? And is not that why you are present,
And happy to be here? Atlas, I weep
To know there is extinct in you the giant
That you repudiated and betrayed,
And so destroyed, when you began with paint.
God, what a sorrow for the stevedores,
I said, beholding you, and then your work.
Smile, if you must. Farewell now to you all.
Please go away."

        "But how, if you are hanged,
And you are dead, and you are still alive,
And are as complimentary as ever,"
Said Lawyer Figg, aware of a new point,
"Are we to act? If you are dead, so be it;
But if you are somehow deceiving us,
And are not irrecoverably deceased,
And if we leave you hanging here alive,
We are accessories."

        "No, you are not,"
Said Pink. "Will you but leave me as I am,
You will be saviors and Samaritans.
Not even in heaven itself, which is not here,
Would there be welcome for the uninvited.
Where are your graces? And in what forgotten

Puddle of dullness have you sunk your tact?
After a decency of hesitation,
And with a tribute of enforced respect,
Two of you might have come; and had you been
Restrained and delicate, and considerate
Of my amelioration and progression,
I should have been as mute and unrebellious
And portable as clay in a wheelbarrow.
When I sought only quiet and privacy,
Why should I be distressed and celebrated
By this obscene inquisitive convocation
Of dry rot walking? I have not summoned
    you,
And cannot save you. There is more law, Figg,
Than you have on your shelves or on your con-
    science;
There is more law than all the colleges
Have heard of, or could make you, if they had
    it,
See to be law. There's music, Evensong,
That might, if you should hear it, overwhelm
The sense of your necessity on earth—
Or all that Amaranth has left of it
For you to trifle with—and humble you
At once to a small heap of sudden dust.
There's a divinity so different, Flax,
From any that man has drafted from the sun,
Or from the seasons, or from the profound
And healing wisdom of his desperation,
That you need sigh no longer for a shadow

That has no substance. You'll be going one day
From this place, which was never the place for
    you;
And when you go, Evensong will assist
With a new elegy that will be no worse
Than any of its innocuous predecessors.
For you, Styx, there's not yet identified
And captured the correct elusive juice
Of action that will combat and extinguish
The potent worms of doubt and indecision
That congregate and feast and multiply
In you as you grow old. In the wrong world
Will you remain till you are carried from it
In a long box; and you will not mind that,
Which is as well.—Will you all go away?
I am not warmed, I am not comforted,
My friends, in your superfluous attention.
Since uninvited you have honored me
With your respective presences, and heard me,
Honor me once again and go away.
For me this visitation is a task
And an embarrassment; and if you discern,
At last, the measure of my disadvantage,
You will not lacerate me to say more.
If this is not enough, and words are nothing,
And a man's final cry to be forgotten
Is less than nothing, you may all be damned.
And Amaranth, in this I'm not omitting
Your new friend Fargo, who has grace at least
To be uneasy and uncomfortable."

"I am not comfortable," said Doctor Styx,
"If that will earn your praise. I am annoyed,
 And uninformed. As one supposed to know,
 I ask: Are you alive, or are you dead?"

"I am as dead as I shall ever be,"
 Said Pink; "and that's as near as a physician
 Requires to know.—Now will you go away?"

"Suspicion," said the Reverend Pascal Flax,
"Whispers to me that in our poet's eyes
 We are not heroes. It may well be so.
 My lost assurances of right and wrong,
 Of true and false, are like a mist that glimmers
 With hidden light. Poets, whatever the end,
 Should know a little more than most of us
 Of our obscurities."

                    Now there were streets again,
And houses—the same streets and the same
        houses
That in his earlier lost wanderings
Alone, Fargo had seen as a place dead,
Or unawakened, till the grave-diggers
Had been a smirch of life that was itself
A sort of death. But now he could see people,
Women and men, who were not horrible,
Or smeared with special evil. Some were young,
Some older, and some very old; and all
Were going somewhere without saying where

Or why to one another, as men went
In lighter places, and with no more sound
Or pageantry of purpose. Amaranth,
Who knew them all, but was unknown to them,
Said presently to Fargo: "At the Tavern,
Where they forget to think, or to count hours,
Their world is right; but thoughts are fickle
    sleepers,
And hours come round. But hours and thoughts
    together
Are not enough to tell them where they are:
They must hear *me;* and only a few do that,
And few that hear will dare an absolution
Of error that is not unsufferable,
For truth untried. My friend, you heard me,
    once,
And dared escape from here. What have you
    done
To fate since then that you are here once more?
There are men so disordered and wrong sighted,
So blind with self, that freedom, when they
    have it,
Is only a new road, and not a long one,
To new imprisonment. But you, my brother,
You are not one of them. You caught yourself
Once in the coiling of a wrong ambition,
And had the quickness to writhe out of it.
You heard me, and you acted, and were free;
And you are here where now there is no freedom.
I shall peruse this mystery to the end;

For some infirmity that sleeps in me
May be a part of it."

               Now there were stairs
Again for them to climb. By the same light
That was not light, and in a swifter way
Than walking, they were in another house.
It was an old house, older than houses are,
Yet somehow not so near as was the first
To always-coming ruin. "All these houses
Will be, as long as there are men and women
To live in them, and die," Amaranth said;
"And that will be as long as there are men
And women." While he said it, they had entered
Another room. There was a woman in it,
Who had white hair, and a young face not young,
And beauty enough to last. Attending her
Was Evensong, who sat and held her hands,
And Ampersand, who was a large black cat.
His name was Ampersand, she said, because
He looked like one when he sat still and held
His tail around him. Amaranth observed
The man and woman who were there together,
And humored them with his unhappy smile;
And Ampersand, who became suddenly
As large as two cats, flung maliciously
A whispered hiss of hate at Amaranth,
Who frowned as if he felt it. Evensong
Let go the lady's hands; and while he held
Her face, he kissed her mouth with all his heart.

"Watchman," he said, "if you and I were young,
We should know better than to be here now.
Was it our doom, or was it our good fate,
That we were not to know?"

                    For Evensong
She had no answer but a laugh. She turned
Her face to Amaranth and smiled agreeably,
Though not as if she must, if she would know
The best of being alive, see more of him.

"Elaine Amelia Watchman, gentlemen,
Who writes, and writes, and writes. You know
    her work,"
Said Evensong; and then to her, "This man
Is Amaranth—which means he is the flower
That never fades. He may sometimes have mur-
    mured
Things in your ears. He is a mighty one
For murmuring; and he murmurs all the time,
To all of us. But most of us who hear him
Believe we are mistaken and hear nothing
But the false voice of doubt, common to man.
You smile because you are afraid of him;
Ampersand spits at him because he hates him—
All for your sake. So the best friend we have
Shall have no thanks, or few. This other fellow,
Who's not here to be happy, is one Fargo,
Who made himself believe he was a painter,
Till Amaranth murmured one day in his ear

[36]

And he escaped. In his right world he learned
That God's good purpose was to make of him
A spring-clean unimpeachable pump-builder—
A foe to phantoms, and a man attuned
To his necessities. And so he was,
Until the free thread of his fate was broken,
Or tangled with another so in a knot
As never to be untied. Now he is here,
And wonders why. And Amaranth wonders
       why;
And when he sets himself to questioning,
Order is hurt, and there are wheels not whirling
Quite the right way. Fargo, it seems, is here
With a perplexed remembrance of his coming,
And with no wish to stay. He has forgotten
How the place looked when he was living in it,
And wonders now if he may not be dead,
And on a sort of halting-ground between
His world and hell, maybe. But he sees wrong,
If that's his picture of us. I may say so,
For I know where we are. Watchman, I wish—
I wish—I do, indeed . . . But no, I won't.
What shall I wish? For I know where I am,
And shall remain. Watchman, ask Amaranth
If you and I were not worth more than art
Before it was a wall we built between us.
Amaranth knows. Whether he tells, or not,
Is his own music. Watchman, I wish to God
That you had never learned to read and write,
And I had never heard of counterpoint.

We might by now be sailing where the whales
Of grief would never catch us."

                                "If it's music
That makes you as you are, play some of yours,"
She said, "and you may suddenly feel better.
Make a sad theme for me—a dismal one
That will be heard when you and I are dust,
And our poor woes are nothing."

                                  "As it happens,"
He answered, brightening, "I have done just
    that;
All but the part of it that shall be heard
When we are dust—which is deplorable,
Though more for the frustration of your wishes
Than of my hopes, which lie where they are
    buried,
And feel already grass-roots tickling them
In a cool sort of way that doesn't hurt.
Amaranth knows; and so does Doctor Styx,
And his uncoffined friends who live because
They know the Tavern and don't know the
    grave.
Here they are now. This Amaranth is a doctor—
A wiser one than Styx—though I suspect
That you had best not make him think of you
Too hard, or let yourself be long concerned
With his prognostic eyes. If they are sorry
For seeing too much that's ominous and lonely

In this place, don't imagine the maternal
In you is to be summoned or excited:
Amaranth is not hungry for a mother,
Though he may be at times preoccupied
With other mothers, and some fathers also,
Who would live longer with their sons and
        daughters
Anywhere else than here—which is a place
To go from with your luggage yet unopened,
And with a ticket that may still be used.
The sorrow of it is that only rarely
Are we to know, until we are too old
Or too unstrung to care, that we are here.
Fargo learned early, and had wings to fly,
But here he is again, without his wings,
And has no story for us. Amaranth
Will have no sleep—I question if he needs it—
Until he knows why Fargo has come back.
If you should ask him, Watchman, you might
        steal
His answer, for you have a stealing voice.
First, here's an elegy for you and me
That may as well be played while there is time
For you to hear it. It is not transcendent,
But you will not forget, if I go first,
That I it was who made it."

                    "Yes," she said,
Smiling a little when it was all over,
"I shall remember it was you who made it.

You will not mind, for I'm not musical,
If that's all I remember."

      "You have ears
That hear with mine, my snowdrop," he said,
  sighing,
And put away his flute: "My wish is only
That you had eyes to see with mine behind you
The lives we two have lost. If I offend,
You learn at last what rancid acrimony
May stew in a sweet nature. It's as well
For you that you are not to visualize
The two we should have been."

      "I see behind me
What I have done. There is my life, up there,—
Almost a shelf of them," she said, and smiled
At Evensong, who looked at Ampersand,
Who glared at Amaranth: "Let others live
And let me write. You must soon go away,
And let me write; and you means all of you.
There's more than has been written."

      "Are you certain
Of that?" asked Amaranth. "Do you know all
That has been written? If you know, your
  knowledge
Might be a pleasure for the unforewarned—
Or possibly might not, if it were printed.
Meanwhile, so far as you are to be read,

[40]

You are not marked or stricken with misgivings
More than are many here. I see no purpose
In our not going. May contentment always
Be near to your command. Farewell; we go."

"Farewell," said Evensong; "and do not see
Too far before you, or too far behind.
God must have made me rather generous,
Or I'd be silent there. Time had the whip,
And you have heard my elegy. Do not say
That it will make death sweet, but say I made it.
So write, and write. See not too far ahead."

"But that's where I will see!" she cried, and ris-
    ing,
Fixed all her fearlessness on Amaranth,
Who said, "But why?"

                    "And I," said Lawyer Figg,
"Can only say with Amaranth, But why?"
"And I," said Doctor Styx, "say only, Why?"
"And I," said Evensong, "say only, Why?"
"And I," said Flax, not caring if he confessed
Accumulating fear, "am asking, Why?"
"I also; I ask, Why?" said Ampersand;
"I can scent presences that you may not,
And emanations that are menacing;
I can feel peril waiting in this room,
Unless you are discreet. 'Twas so in Egypt."
Fargo said nothing, but remained apart,

A stranger trembling with expectancy
And sightless apprehension.

                         Lawyer Figg
Implored her with a look, and said, "Dear friend,
You have heard Ampersand. Will you hear me?
Four of us here you know, and you know well
What time has made of us. What you behold
Is not ourselves, but whims and caricatures
Of our mishandled heritage. We may say,
And with no unsubstantial arrogance,
Or thin defense of our lost usefulness,
That in the proper light of our beginning
We shone for more than this. And as we are,
There may be more of us than we reveal;
We make a tinkling jest of the wrong road
That brought us here, but when we are alone
We put the bells away. Say, if you will,
That we are for a moment here alone
Together, and do your wisest to believe.
Believe that you do best in seeing as far
Before you as tomorrow; and tomorrow—
As far as one day more. Ask Ampersand,
And he will tell you so."

                    "My learned friend
Says well," said Doctor Styx. "Your life, you
    say,
Is in your work. Why then, in God's name,
    Madam,

Should you not have your life, and leave to others
The joy of twisting and tormenting theirs?
There are no enemies present, or abroad,
I dare affirm, to thwart you or molest you.
Why then should you be curious, or impatient?
And why not leave the pool unvisited
Until the angel comes? Why trouble it now?
Peril is here, but only if you seek it;
There's no distinguishable jeopardy
That's imminent in your mortal organism;
You have, or so it looks, a competence;
You have a place to live; you have your tea;
You have your books; you have a stately cat;
You have, in sum, so far more than is frequent
In this infected realm, that I beseech
And beg of you to see as far before you
As you see now, and say no more about it.
Ask Ampersand, and he will tell you so."

"Dear lady," said the Reverend Pascal Flax,
"You have heard physic, you have heard the law.
Now let this humble and unworthy tongue
Tell solemnly to you a piercing message,
Which I have heard and have interpreted,
Perforce and clearly, as the voice of God.
Of late I seldom hear it as it sounded
Once on a time, but now I'm filled and ringing,
I swear, as I am here, with truth not mine.
My words, I fear, would be for you as chaff,
Or like a dust of language. Pray forget

[43]

Remonstrance, and believe a voice that warns you
That you will see no farther. Be at peace
With time; for in this region where we are,
There is no other peace. Ask Ampersand,
And he will tell you so."

                    She laughed at him,
But a brave terror living in her eyes
Would not be mirth: "You are all trying to
     scare me,
And that's not why I like you. If you ask him,
Evensong, who has no persuasion left,
And will be happier for not having it,
Will tell you that although I am not large,
There's in me an insistent little spirit
That holds and shields me from life-eating
     trifles—
Love, doubt, regret, or fear. I'm never vague;
I never cloud myself with airy vapors.
When I am dust, my work will say all this,
And against all your doubts. I should not say
     it,
But I can see not one here to assure you,
Except myself, that I'm beyond a fear
Of Amaranth, or of anything in his words,
Or in his eyes. Come—let me see those eyes
That are so famous. I like things that are famous,
If only they're not frauds. Where's Pink the
     poet?
I felt one that I missed."

         "We left him hanging,"
Said Evensong. "He told himself, as you do,
That he was not afraid of Amaranth's eyes;
And so he looked, and saw himself in them
As he was really."

        "I am not surprised,"
She said, "and in a manner am not sorry.
I could have told him his enameled words
Were dead while he was making puzzles of
      them.
Sometimes, when I was tired, I played with them,
But never read them twice in the same way.
And some of them were beautiful. Poor fellow!
He never found his world."

        "I am not certain,"
Said Doctor Styx, "that there was ever a world
For him to find. If so, I have not seen it.
He saw me as a stripped materialist,
And may have known. And Amaranth, if he
      knows,
Will never tell us. If we knew too much,
And the bright armor of our own esteem
Were torn from us, we might all be embarrassed.
Madam, remember that."

        "I'm tired of *that!*"
She cried; and rushing at Amaranth, she seized
      him.

[45]

"Who are you! Look at me—look—look!" she
    said,
  And sought his eyes with hers. His arms were
    folded
  While she was looking, and his arms were folded
  While she came staggering away from him,
  With Evensong to guide her as he might
  The blind and silent. She would see no chair,
  But stood taut and erect against her table,
  Pressing with her cold hands the edge of it.

"Nothing is half so hard," he said to her,
"As learning first to know. Think of what's left.
  Here is the book of yours that you like best.
  Listen: I'll read a page that will be read
  When you and I are dust."

                       She turned her face,
  And watched him with a fear that made of it
  Almost a face that never had been hers,
  While he removed a volume, richly bound,
  And held it, waiting. "Listen," he said, "and
    smile."
  He opened it, and found between the covers,
  Where leaves had been, only gray flakes of dust
  That fluttered like thick snow and on the floor
  Lay silent. A thin scream came out of her,
  And there was nothing more. She was not there.
  Where she had been there was a little mound
  Of lighter dust, and that was all there was.

"I think," said Evensong, "that she had always,
Hidden somewhere within her, unacknowledged,
A sort of love for me. With your permission,
I'll say she is mine, now." With careful hands
He put it all in a small envelope
And sealed it with his ring. And then he said,
"If she had stayed, she might have learned too
    soon
Where she was living, and why she was here.
There was no resignation born within her.
Truth, coming first as an uncertainty,
Would have said death to her, and would have
    killed her
Slowly. Now I shall have her with me always.
Forgive me if I go away, my friends,
And for a while am silent and alone."
He paused, and with a last look at the place
Where she had been so long, he walked away;
And after him walked Ampersand the cat,
Crying as if bewildered and forgotten.

"Well, Fargo, my new friend, my new old
    friend,"
Said Amaranth, "what do you make of this?
Are you not sorry to be here again?
For this is where you were before you heard
My voice and fled. But that was years ago,
And there's no going now. Well, if you must.
We understand you, and are not amazed
That you and Evensong should for a time

Seek a seclusion and a retrospect.
But have a memory and a care, my friend;
Remember there are still the grave-diggers,
And do not go too far from here alone."

III

Now there were graves. There were so many of
    them
That they were like a city where tall houses
Were shrunken to innumerable mounds
Of unremembered and unwindowed earth,
Each holding a foiled occupant whose triumph
In a mischosen warfare against self
And nature was release. "If I had stayed,"
Said Fargo to the desolate still acres
Between him and a line that might have been
His last horizon, "I might be by now
The wrong inhabitant of a cold home
As dark as one of these." He thought of that,
And hurried fast along. "I fled the place,
And was for years safe and away from it,
With only memories of a young mistake
To make it real. Then why am I here now?
For I am here—still here." He thought of that,
And hurried faster. Where he might be going
He did not ask, and there were none to tell him;
There was no sign to show him. There was
    nothing
But graves, which he had passed with Amaranth
Before they found the Tavern, and those houses

That never could be far enough behind him
Until he knew that Amaranth and his eyes
Were nowhere watching him.

                        But he must fix
His will, with no more waste of memory
Or thought, on his one purpose of escape
From this insidious region of illusions
That once had made of him their prisoner,
And then had let him go. He had come back
For reasons unrevealed, and had been driven,
Out of time's orbit into a lost chaos
Where time and place were tossed and flung
      together
Like an invisible foam of unseen waves;
He had come back to a doom recognized
As one to fly from, and now he was flying.
As he rushed on he felt his heart within him
Pounding as if with a foreboding joy
For liberty that was not yet to be his;
But surely somewhere far ahead of him,
If he pursued it and saw not behind him,
Nor thought of what there was that followed
     him,
Nothing—not Amaranth even, he conceived—
Would hold him in his frenzy for return
To his right world where he had learned to know
That he was living there, and was not dying
Of slow deceit—which, even while it killed,
Whispered and leered, and pointed still the way,

So rarely taken, to deliverance.
But he had seized it; he had heard a voice
Above the whisper, and he had obeyed it;
And in obedience he had found release.
Why then should he be here among the dead?
Was it all graves—this half remembered home
Of ghosts and young ambitions and regrets?
Was he the only fugitive thing alive
Among so many dead? He paused enough
To wonder, and then heard an aged voice
Beside him, as if someone buried there
Were speaking to him.

        "Come with me," it said;
"Or better, remain with me a while, and rest.
There'll be no sailing yet. We shall be early,
And still have time for rest. Your name is Fargo.
I know you. You are the nimble prisoner
Who fled from here while time would let you go.
I saw you in the Tavern, where they told me
Of your return. Why in God's ancient name,
My hurrying friend, have you returned? And
      where
Would you be going so fast among the graves?
In this one lies a woman. If I killed her,
She suffered on a slow and loving rack
That hid from me its name. For I was blind—
Until it was too late; and then I saw.
I was a long time learning where I was,
Though I heard murmurs."

                              Fargo, looking down,
Saw sitting at a mound, long overgrown
With negligence, a figure less infirm
Than it was indigent of enterprise.
Gray-haired and wrinkled, he looked up at Fargo,
And smiled at him with eyes that held a fire
More like the shine of burnt-out stars far off,
And shining still, than it was like man's life.
"You do not know me; and there's no remorse
For you in that," he said. "Your ignorance
Of my oblivion is excusable
As one more of those planetary trifles
For which we are not scorned or persecuted.
I'm Ipswich, the inventor. I have never
Invented anything that you have heard of,
But God, the dreams I've had! When I was
      young,
Visions already of quick miracles,
That would be mine, were like a fire inside me,
Set there to burn with God's immortal fuel
Till all my dreams were deeds, and my ambi-
      tions
A time-defying monument of glory
For me and for my science, and for my toil
In darkness where the light was always coming
For men, my brothers. But as one by one,
After soul-wrenching search and repetition,
And after years of it, there would come rays
That almost would be light—so, one by one,
The rays would always fade; and somewhere else

There would be crowns and wreaths and pil-
    grimages
That were not made for me. Another man's
    flame
Would have been kindled with accomplishment,
And in the path of its illumination
Would quench my gleam for ever. And so it
    was—
Not once, but for as many times as fire
Within would burn my doubts to sodden ashes.
A stranger, burning with more fire than mine,
And seeing with eyes that had more light be-
    hind them,
Would find at last, where my eyes were not
    searching,
One waiting treasure more for the world's crown
Of common glory. She who is lying here
So quietly, and with no untold reproach,
Never complained. She only smiled and
    starved—
Partly for constant and too far prolonged
Frugalities of home, partly for me.
I loved her more than life, but less than science.
She knew the last; the first I never told her—
Although she may have known. I think she did,
For I remember how she looked at me,
And found no fault. I can remember too
A doubt that had an ambush in her eyes,
And would peer out at me when she forgot;
Which was all natural. For a woman's view

Of heaven at home is not one of her waiting
Always, and on the watch, for a concealed
Fulfilment that she knows will never come.
I know it; and if I had known it then,
I do not say my sorrow for it now
Would show me it was not the fate of nature
That I should have been Ipswich. There's a
    casting
Of too much hallowed and long-honored non-
    sense
Over the names and skeletons of all those
Who might as well have been George Washing-
    ton
As not. But this, I fear, accuses me;
For truth on crutches is a mendicant,
Though God be at her side supporting her.
But there's another glimpse I get of her,
Wherein she stands imperious and intact.
I do not say she points a finger at me,
But there's a frowning that I cannot like
On her calm face, and there is in her eyes
A look that penetrates and troubles me;
For always when it finds me I must hear
Remembered murmurings of a still voice,
Less pleasing and less welcome than a sound
Of anything seen could be. For the long years
It followed me, I stifled it with lies,
Trying to tell myself there was no voice;
But there it was. There was an ear within me
That always heard it, if these ears would not.

I cannot hear it now; and silence tells
To me the reason, which is old and easy:
The voice believes that I'm already dead,
And seeks the living who would still be warned.
But I know better. There's a ship that sails
Today, and you and I shall be on board,
Soon to be leaving, far and far behind us,
A world of graves that are the fame and harvest
Of reaping what should never have been sown."

"I know the murmur of the voice you heard,"
Said Fargo, "and I know whose voice it was;
For I was one of the permitted few
That out of a loud chorus of delusion
Sifted and heeded it. I fled this place,
And found another, where I found myself.
Why am I here? God knows. I have not done
Large evil in the world where I belong;
I am not here for that; I am not here
By wilful choice, by call, or by command
That I remember."

        The inventor smiled,
And rising, winced with age: "No matter now,
For we shall soon be sailing. It's as well,
Sometimes, that we leave reasons in the darkness
Where they like best to live. We do not know
So many forces that are moulding us
That we must have a word we call a name
For more, say, than a few of them." He laughed

[55]

At Fargo silently, and without sound
He disappeared; and there were no more graves.

Now there were ships and silent wharves again,
And a black water lying like a floor
That he might walk away on till he found
The freedom he had lost. Fargo at first
Saw naught that had a motion or a shadow
Of life. Where there was neither night nor day,
There were no shadows; and where life was not,
There was no motion. He could see below him
The dark flood that had once invited him,
But did not now. If there was any escape,
He knew it was not there; and in his knowing
He owned unwillingly a nameless debt
To Amaranth. He wondered what it was,
And might have tired his wits not finding it,
Had he come not so near to losing them
Just then, when faintly from a rusted funnel
Not far away from him he saw smoke rising
Into an empty silence. There was life
Somewhere; and it was in a battered thing
Of rust and iron that had been a ship,
And here in its last port had floated only
Because it had not sunk. Now the smoke rose
And rolled itself into a solid soot
That scattered and spread imperceptibly
Into a distant cloud; and out of cabins,
Which he had fancied might have been the home
Of sleeping demons, there came noisily

A swarm of superannuated men
Who sang with shattered voices, and of women,
Obscenely decked and frescoed against time,
Who shrilled above the men deliriously
A chorus of thanksgiving and release.
Each man and woman held a shaking goblet,
From which there dripped or spilled a distillation
Of unguessed and unmeasured potency,
Which had already vanquished any terrors
Attending embarkation, and all sorrows
Inherent in farewell.

           Fargo, alone
With his amazement, felt lost recollections
Of words returning that were spoken once,
And were forgotten. An old man had said
A ship would sail away, and he had vanished.
No, the same man was here. Ipswich himself,
The old inventor, was approaching him,
And holding with an outstretched trembling hand
A dripping goblet. Fargo pushed away
The fevered invitation and said, "Ipswich,
What are you doing with a drink like this?
I do not know it, but your frenzy tells me
It is no drink for man. Throw it away,
And come with me."

          "Come where with you—and why!"
The old man cried. "No drink for man or
    woman,

[57]

You say, and you say well. We are not men—
We are not women. Since I made this drink,
We are the souls of our misguided selves,
And our lives are no longer our disasters.
We are immortal now, and we are going
Where life will cease to be the long mistake
That we have made of it. We have no captain,
But we have a rejuvenated sailor,
Who never loved the ocean, to command us;
After a measure of this drink of mine,
He sings to me of a world built for us
Dim leagues away, and says he can hear billows
Roaring on undiscovered promontories.
And we have an indignant engineer,
Who should have been a surgeon, driving us
Out of this world anon and to another,
Where long ago, could we have seen ourselves
With eyes that we have now, we should have
    lived
And grown to glory that shall still be ours.
Come, come with us! There is no other way.
Drink this that I have made and brought for you,
And come! Oh come, for we shall soon be sail-
    ing,
And we shall not come back. Praise be to God,
We are not coming back!"

                    The old inventor,
Suffused with an ecstatic saturation,
Proffered again the trembling glass to **Fargo**,

Who learned, with an incredulous reluctance,
That he was worse than tempted; he was help-
    less.
There was a diabolical bouquet
Enveloping and intoxicating him,
As if a siren that he could not feel
Or see were breathing in his arms. He faltered;
But when the old man smiled again, he saw
The wisest and the most affectionate
Of guardian fathers reassuring him,
And urging him to drink if he would live.

"Take it, my son," he said, "and come with
    me,
Where we shall be defrauded never more
By the grief-plundered and pernicious dreams
That have defeated us. Drink it, my son.
Trust Ipswich, the inventor. Do you see me
As a false comrade, as a man of peril?
Or as a vicious remnant of disaster
Who might inveigle, for his wretched pleasure,
Others to his damnation? There are many
Who sink so far that they may go no lower,
And there may be content. If they are so,
May God reveal to them what they have done,
I say, and let them suffer what they see.
Have I the features or the inward manner
Of an insatiable depravity?
I should be inconsolable to believe it.
Drink, drink, my son!"

                            Fargo seized eagerly
The dripping glass and its infernal fragrance,
And would have swallowed the perfidious
        draught
It held, believing it the wine of life,
Had not a power like that of a calm hand,
Holding him and compelling him to pause,
Touched him and driven a chill of knowledge
        through him
That made him see. He saw the old inventor
Now as a poor decrepit frail fanatic,
With gentle madness gleaming out of him
Instead of pleasant life. He threw away
The glass, and heard it breaking.

                            "No," he said,
And laughed at the old man indulgingly:
"I'd rather be the last fool left ashore
Than be afloat with you. What wits are mine
Will be some company; and if I conserve them,
There may be a way out. If there's a way
Without a wreck before the end of it,
There's also, and for all there is of me,
The task of finding it. If your invention
Has crowned itself at last with desperation,
Say it is yours and leave to me despair.
For me it is the safer of the two,
And is not always a fixed incubus."

The old man shook his head at him, and wept:

"My son, it is the very fiend and father
Of lies who makes himself invisible
Before he tells you this, and lets you say it.
Despair, or desperation—what you will—
There is no safety here. Come, come with me,
Before it is too late! Come, and be saved!
For we are going now—far, far away
From this imprisonment that was our folly,
And was almost our grave. You will not come?
God save you, then. You know not what you
    do.
Farewell, farewell, my son. I gave release
For you to drink, and I could give no more.
Farewell, farewell."

               The old man sang those words
To Fargo for as long as he went shaking
Back to the crowded hulk where men and women
Still waved their hands and sang. There was a
    puff
Of white steam and a sound of a thin whistle,
And then that ruin of what was once a ship
Struggled and groaned like a sick beast of bur-
    den
That asked of man only some solitude
Wherein to sleep and die. Driven to move
By some last artifice of mind and action,
It left the desolate wharf where Fargo waited,
Watching it as it labored helplessly
Away with a sad clanking, and more groaning,

And a great hissing. Smoke and steam were leak-
    ing
Infernally and impossibly through plates
Where time and rust had eaten them; and now
There was a dark eruption all at once
Of smoke and sudden flame from a tall funnel
That leaned before it fell; and all on board
Were singing so that Fargo on the wharf
Could hear their sound of joy—till a dull roar
Became a silence, and there was no ship,
And no more sound.

       "Their voyage was not a long one,
Though longer than we might have prophesied,"
Amaranth said, behind him. Fargo turned
And found a patient face, familiar now,
Watching as if no more had happened there
Than a man going home: "It seems a pity,
My friend, but there is no way out of here
Alive like that. There's no such easy stealth,
Nor such abrupt and festive exodus
As your mad friend foresaw. You would have
    drunk
Your doom in his invention, had I let you,
And would have gone with him where others
    went
Who are gone now indeed. Their vanities,
And their Plutonian amenities,
Were not long to endure. Are you not glad
That I was here in time?"

                    "I don't know that,"
Said Fargo, after thought. "If I am here
To stay until I die, and for no reason,
I am not sure that my friend's last invention
Was not the true release he said it was."

"Was that his name for it?" Amaranth asked.
"I wonder how he knew. How do men learn
  To know, and where the light is none too
        clear,
  The language of so much that's unrevealed
  And ultimate in the books they have not read?
  I see that here I must have some instruction."

"Is that why you are smiling—if you call it
  A smile that you are wearing?" Fargo asked.
"Do you smile always when a crazy ship
  Is blown to pieces, and all those on board
  Are blown to death, or drowned?'"

                    "Not always—no,"
Amaranth said, and gazed away from Fargo
To where the ship had been: "But I see now
Nothing that holds us longer where we are.
This is a place that I have never sought,
Or fancied. There is no escape this way;
And you, if you are shrewd and sound, will
        hasten
Away from here with me."

                         Now there were ships
And silent wharves no longer, and no music
Of those intoxicated emigrants
Who sang no more. Now there were only walls
And web-hung rafters, and a patched north win-
    dow
That was half covered with as much as time
Had left of a stained curtain. On a floor
More famous than the man who never swept it,
There was an easel with a picture on it,
And a few sorry chairs. In one of them
Sat Atlas, with his red shirt and his beard,
Admiring audibly a last achievement,
Which of itself would be a revolution
When the world heard of it. He said it would;
And pouring a stout drink from a full bottle,
He said it twice. He swore at Lawyer Figg
With a voluminous harmless blasphemy
That ended innocently with a laugh
Of patient pity, whereat the lawyer smiled
For sudden lack of words to fill the moment.

"The gifted have their obligations, Atlas,"
He ventured, "and are lenient when a lawyer
Requires a breath of time to stroke his chin
And hesitate. I don't know what I think,
And you don't care. Your manner makes a riot
For an uncertain eye. It agitates
And dazzles; and I'm only a poor layman,
Too old now to be learning a new language

That has no roots. You say it is a horse,
And I have never called it a volcano.
You say the sky is blue, and so it is,
And a horse has a right to some of it;
But when you make him indigo all over,
And then forget that you leave out of him
Everything that I've always called a horse,
A lawyer wonders why it is a horse,
Whatever the sky may be. Green trees are blue,
Sometimes—I know they are, for I have seen
    them—
But even blue trees have roots."

                    "Oh, damn your trees,
And damn your roots," roared Atlas, angrily.
"You'll eat a poisoned rat if you say 'roots'
To me again, by God!"

                    "Dear, dear," said Flax.
"Why such an animal accent? By your leave,
I'll ask for silence while I drink to peace,
Atlas, and its concomitant, good will.
When you are on the westward side of life,
Which man's imagination has for ages
Configurated aptly as a mountain,
You will have learned, and by some sore tuition,
That peace, if you are chosen to achieve it,
Is worth a world of noise. Sinners of old
Believed if they prayed once or twice to God,
He would prepare for them an easy march

To heaven without good works; and nowadays
Sinners in art believe there are short roads
To glory without form. I drink once more
To peace and to good will, and to you, Atlas;
And now it is a horse. If lesser men
Deny it, say the Reverend Pascal Flax—
A clergyman decayed, who might have been
A lawyer, or perchance a politician—
Beseeches them to tell him what it is
If it is not a horse."

              "I was not raised
In your world, Reverend," Atlas answered,
     growling,
"And I can't tell you all that's in my heart
To say to you. I could tell Styx and Figg
Where they might go, together or separately,
But there's a broadcloth line that I respect—
Though I don't see that you, with all your roots,
Have a plantation on your side of it."

"Your pardon, gentlemen"; said Amaranth,
"But there are waves of latent indignation
Coming from Atlas that you may not feel.
He may be large and dark and powerful,
But strength and size have sensibilities
That may deceive."

           "There are so many in him,"
Said Doctor Styx, who now possessed the bottle,

"That color with him is all, and needs no line.
He says there is one line that he respects;
And I wish, Atlas—here's to your long life—
I wish to God that there were more of them.
I am less exercised and less excited
Because your horse is blue, than I am, Atlas,
Because you see it and still see a horse.
Like my contemporaries, Flax and Figg,
I lean to less rebellious innovations;
And like them, I've an antiquated eye
For change too savage, or for cataclysms
That would shake out of me an old suspicion
That art has roots. Atlas, why do you flash
A look like that at me for not yet saying,
In friendship, that a blue horse, or a green one,
Should have at least a buried line somewhere
To say it is a horse? Creators ache,
I fear, for growing too fast; and I am sorry
For you, that in your frenzy to attain
You have found only one line to respect—
The which, being broadcloth on a clergyman,
Is rather a step away from a blue horse.
And what am I, meanwhile? A stranded leech,
Of no announced importance or repute,
Whose word has an authority in art
As large as yours in physic. To you, Atlas,
I drink, and to the swelling of your fame
For centuries, till it says farewell to earth,
And floats above it like a firm balloon.
The more I drink, the more I see a horse,

[67]

And love him none the less for being blue.
What do I see, if it is not a horse?
If anyone says it's not, say Doctor Styx
Challenges them to call it anything else.
I shall remain here neighing until I know
Why it is not. If it is not a horse,
What else, in God's name, is it?"

                              "Hear him, Atlas,"
Said Evensong. "Hear him, and humor him;
And heed him as you would the silver noise
Of poplars in a breeze. I take your word;
And when you say to me it is a horse,
To me it is a horse. Why call a storm
From nowhere, when we may as well have peace?
Our reverend friend is right in prizing it
Higher than controversy. For myself,
I'm a too long unwanted votary
Of old and overworn deficiencies;
I thought once that a multitude of notes,
Because they were my creatures, must be music.
I should have been perhaps a naturalist.
Had nature won, I should know more of horses;
And of art, possibly."

                        "Good God!" said Atlas,
Pouring a giant's drink and gulping it,
"Your soft way of not saying what you're afraid
  To say, and your sweet throwing of your own
      failures

Into my face to keep me company,
Will not go down. Your motive, I dare say,
Is to be kind. Well, put your kindness back
Into your windpipe. Someone else may want it.
There are some hungry souls that are so sick
With having nothing but the past to live on,
That like as not they'll eat the withered skins
Of cant you throw to them, and thank you for
　　them.
Now I begin to see. If God's alive,
He must be laughing to watch Evensong
Pouring his patronizing oily pity
On Me. My God, on Me! I've pitied you
Too long, and I have never let you know it."

He shook himself like a large dog and laughed
With inward indignation and amazement;
Then, swallowing what was left, he disap-
　　peared—
Soon to arrive again triumphantly,
Emerging fiercely from behind a screen
With a new bottle. With a nervous hand
He drew the cork, and paused before he drank:
"Now I begin to see. You, Evensong,
Are not alone. There's you, Figg—and you,
　　Styx—
And, Reverend, there's you. I've always liked
　　you;
I've liked your talk, and I've liked your not
　　seeing

The difference that I felt. I don't forget,
But that's no use today. I know you all
Today, and should have known you long ago.
You're all alike. You all think I'm a fool.
Because God gave me vision to see more
Than you know how to see, there's nothing left
For you to do but laugh. The fool's old laugh
At everything that's not yet cracks and cob-
    webs
Will never frighten me. It's the true cross,
And always has been, that we have to bear.
Was I a stevedore? Well, if I was,
Once on a time there was a Carpenter;
And some of you have heard what happened to
    him.
It was a portion of my preparation
To be a stevedore, and that part's over.
I was a good one, if that's any matter,
And I've a strong arm still. If I should use it,
I might throw all of you, and never feel it
Afterwards, one by one out of the window—
All but you, Amaranth. I don't know you.
I don't know what you are, or what you think.
But if you fancy I'm afraid of you,
There'll have to be some showing. You and
    your friend—
Your new friend Fargo, who tried once to paint,
And then, in answer to God's call, made pumps—
Are silent over there. You are all silent . . .
Well, Reverend, have a drink, if you won't talk.

I thought so. It was not my fate, when young,
To go your delicate ways, but I know men;
And, Reverend, I know you. And I know
  paint—
Which is what you don't know. I mean all
  present—
All but you, Amaranth. I don't know you;
And I'm not certain . . . Maybe I'll stop there.
Pink said he didn't like you, to your face,
But I'm not saying just that. Only a poet
Would have such a divine be-damned assurance.
It's not that I don't like you. I don't know
  you . . .
Evensong, have a drink, and let's forget it.
I see that I'm not done with Amaranth,
Who still believes that he can feel inside him
A sort of squirming notion, or suspicion,
That I'm afraid of him. I'll drink to him,
Just to convince him that I'm not afraid—
Of him, or any man."

   "I have not heard
The sound yet of one timid syllable
From you," said Amaranth. "If you uttered one,
I should be disconcerted and reduced
Unpleasantly to many questionings.
To make myself unwelcome, I could wish,
Meanwhile, and only for your peace and reason,
For thunder not so loud. Faith, if assured,
Will ride without a cannon or a banner—

On a blue horse, if it be necessary—
As far as there's a way. I like to fancy
That your explosive note of confidence
Today has more the tone of celebration
Than of a sounding habit."

                    "You have words
That I can't play with," Atlas answered, thickly;
"I went to my own school, and have some reading
Locked up in me that I don't advertise;
For I've a rough tongue still. I know it's rough;
But I can make it say, and without oil,
That I'm as ready as a rat for cheese
To meet whatever it is that you are hiding,
And see myself today among the masters.
Where are they? Bring them on. I'll say to
    them,
Or maybe to as many as I've an eye for,
That we are brothers. And they'll say to me,
'Brothers we are.' And they'll shake hands with
    Atlas."

Amaranth looked a long time at the bottle,
And then away: "I wish, for your sake, Atlas,
That your vociferous demon had his being
Only in what you drink. But he was in you
Before the grain that angers him was planted.
Well, peace be with you, Atlas. If I stay
Till you may know me better, there's that matter
Of liking me, remember. For my part,

I would have only peace—if peace were mine
To make, or share."

        "Stay where you are!" growled Atlas.
"You are not going away with your conceit
To keep you warm and to leave me a fool
Behind you. Where are those damned eyes of
     yours
That Flax and Figg and Styx and Evensong—
And Pink, poor devil—have seen, to see them-
     selves?
Let me look into them and find what's there.
You are afraid—for me? My God!—for Me?
You are worth living for. If I don't laugh,
I'll need a drink to keep myself polite."

He took an ample swallow, and then laughed
At Amaranth, who stood with folded arms
Against the wall, and said: "I have not asked
For this; and Atlas, it is not too late
For me to go . . . You will, then?"

                Atlas laid
His large and hairy hands on Amaranth,
And gazed into his eyes. There was no need
Of words when the collapse of everything
That had been Atlas fell into the chair
Before the picture—to sit there and shake
And be a speechless wreck till it arose
And said to Amaranth: "Who is this God

[73]

That I have heard of who saves men? Where is
    he?
Let me look once into his face and tell him
What he has done to me! If you are God,
Amaranth, you had better have been the Devil.
What are you? Are you . . ."

                    "No, I am not God;
And I am not the Devil," Amaranth said.
"And you, in your first waking, are not Atlas.
You are a stranger, still to meet yourself,
Alone and unafraid."

                    "Afraid? By heaven
And hell! Afraid of what!" Out of his clothes
He drew a sailor's knife, and opened it:
"See this; and try to see now, as I shall,
    The blood run where I strike. The blood you see
    Will be my life, and all that my life means."
He slashed the picture lengthwise and crosswise
    Till there was nothing but shreds left of it.
"Now say that I'm afraid."

                    "Why make me say it?"
Amaranth asked. "This is no joy for me.
If you were not afraid of me, my friend,
Your faith would not have cared enough to look
Into my eyes—and you would not be here.
If doubt had not been living like a worm
Within you, Atlas, you would not be here.

You would be in a world where clearer voices
Would be less mine than yours. Clearer, because
Men hear mine to forswear it and forget it,
And say it never was—which is not, Atlas,
The same as knowing they have never heard it.
There is still time for you to go from here.
Many awake to learn that they are born
Out of a dream. There may be a new region
Waiting for you outside, and far from here,
Where I shall have no power to trouble you."

"Good God, is there no truth left anywhere!"
  Cried Atlas. "How many times have you been
        born,
  Amaranth? Six or seven? The pain, they say,
If we remembered it, is worse than dying.
I don't mind death. I mind the falling down
Of a tall monument that I was building
Higher than lightning, and as everlasting
As man on earth. To your health, Amaranth!
And may you live to be the curse of man
As long as earth breeds life."

                          So saying, he poured
A fearsome drink, and laughed when it was gone.
Then he said, swaying. "Where is your new
        world
For me? The only world that I have had
Is gone now. You have made a desert of it,
Amaranth; and the rest of you are liars—

You and your learning, and your ways of saying
To me that I'm an outcast and a fool.
What are you all to me? I know you now.
I know you, and I see you—all alike.
You are not much to see. The fire of lies
That lit the way for me to find no more
Than you here at the end of it was wasted.
I thought it was the lamp of God. What was it?
And what was I? I don't know who I am.
I haven't even a name. Does anyone care?
Now see what I shall do. And if you say,
Before you see, that I'm afraid to know,
Say it—and see!"

            He seized another canvas,
Slashing it madly, and then seized another,
And still another, until not one of them
Was left unsacrificed. "Good-bye," he said;
And now he was half hidden by the screen.
"Amaranth, you have done a good day's work.
Good-bye, and damn your soul." He disap-
    peared;
And there was nothing seen or heard of Atlas
Till there was an explanatory sound
Of weight that fell down heavily on the floor.

"You, Styx, are a physician," Amaranth said;
"And if your various means and implements
Of restoration are not here, no matter.
There is no need for more of us than you

To see him; and you need not stay with him
Longer than you are pleased with his appear-
  ance."

"I shall regret for life," said Evensong,
"My footless notion of preparing him
For resignation—or for God knows what.
Pity and condescension dress themselves
Adroitly in humility's old clothes,
And may as well be naked."

                    "Let your motive
Be more the salvage of your memory there
Than your mistake. Your qualm is not uncom-
  mon,"
Said Amaranth: "Well, Fargo, my old friend,
Where do you go this time? The grave-diggers
Are never so far from here but they may find
  you;
And they remember. If you like my counsel,
You will avoid them; for I may not always
Be where you are when you have lost your way."

IV

Now there were glimmering walls that were to
    Fargo
At the same time familiar and unknown.
Once he had worked in such a place, he knew,
But this room was not his—though it revealed
Appearances that had the ghostliness
Of old possessions that were memories;
And here, against the protest of his being
And will, he was compelled again to paint.
He wondered why; and Evensong, who sat
On high there with a willing weariness
Of one who would do anything for a friend,
Was asking with a still defeated smile
Fargo's unanswered question.

                              "If, like you,
I had escaped from here when first I heard
The voice of Amaranth, I would more than rather
Have worn my feet off running than come back,"
Said Evensong: "If I had built my house
In the right world instead of no house here,
I should have locked it so that no invaders
From a deceiving past, like yours and mine,

[78]

Should have crept in to drag me out of it,
And carry me back to this. If I had found
Myself where I belonged, and not too late
For my indifference to be interested,
I should have stayed. I should have let the Devil
Do his own tinkling, and been satisfied
Not to be scoring for him, with him grinning
Here in the dark. I should have been content
With hearing what there's more than life has
      time for
Without the blameless help of my small off-
      spring.
If I'm in any measure truculent,
Or too censorious, they are not suffering.
Did they not give me hours and years enough
Of indecisions and uncertainties
Before I told them I was not their father,
And that their mother was the Devil's playmate?
Unlike some accidents of ecstasy,
They made me think they clamored to be born.
You know their argument, and their revenge.
Wherefore, I fear that I'll ask endlessly,
My valued and unfathomable friend,
Why in God's name, having got once out of
      this,
To the firm highways of deliverance,
Have you come back? If you should paint me,
      Fargo,
For twice as many days as there are hours
In this one, you'd have then, as heaven's wages,

AMARANTH

A failure maybe not so nullifying
As death, nor yet so luring that even love
Would climb a mountain more than once to see
    it.
Fargo, if I could put my tongue to sleep,
It would still talk, and say, Why, Why, and
    Why
Have you come back?"

                    "If I could answer you,"
Said Fargo, painting on with a compulsion
That had no pleasure in it, and no faith,
"I could say whose offense and whose resentment
Has will that I have not. It's like a dream
Of going back to school, and to old lessons
That once we thought were learned. There is
    no place
Left here for me. Has Amaranth any name
For labor that compels an execution
Because it wills itself against our wits?
I've toiled where effort was intelligible
In circumstances I would not have chosen;
And I have chosen error that afterwards
Rejected me and let me save myself;
But here there is no choice. There is no heart
In me for this; and there is none in you.
When I am seasoned and acclimated
Like you, beyond escape or thought of it,
I may know why it is that you are smiling;
I may—if death forgets me for so long."

[80]

"It comes all to the heart, and to the treasure—
Which is adjacent, or synonymous,"
Said Evensong. "I knew a fellow once,
An ablest of the ineffectuals—
One of the brotherhood, and extant yet—
Whose qualities had so many focuses
That there was never a sure centre for them.
So he became impatient and unruly,
And fixed upon a last determination
To finish it all with drink. But there he failed,
As always; for his heart was never in it,
He said. He still lives, and he drinks enough,
But not sufficient for incineration;
And all because his heart was never in it.
So, Fargo, now you know why you must fail
In painting me. Your heart is somewhere else,
And there your treasure is. It is not here."

"No," Fargo answered; "it is far from here.
Yet Atlas would have said that his was here.
If not, where was it? There was nothing in life
For him but art; and when he saw the end
That had been waiting for him, there was not
        life."

"Better say paint than art," said Evensong.
"Color with him, when he discovered it,
    And learned a little of its perilous ways,
    Was a long drunkenness—which he conceived
    As new, and revolution. While it rumbled,

[81]

He should have learned to draw. But like some
    others,
Assured of more than they possessed, he flung
His first bomb to annihilate for ever
Those ancient superfluities of line
And form that were an obstacle between him
And his desire. There was a blast of color,
And Atlas never knew that he was blind
Until he knew the eyes of Amaranth.
It may have been as well. He might have seen
His end too soon; and his awakening
Might have been longer torture for the man
Than Amaranth and his eyes. His wits were
    sharp,
And though they were untempered by the world,
They still possessed an edge that would have
    turned
Itself against him as it did today.
He was a victim, or a sport, of glory
That would have laughed him mad. Amaranth
    said
His doubt was living in him like a worm;
But I should have said sleeping. Does it matter?"

"I'm searching my last archive to find out
What matters, or what doesn't," Fargo answered,
"If I am to stay here. Have you not found
One door yet that will open? I'm so far
From all I left behind me that was right,
That I'll be wondering somewhat if I'm dead,

And in a sort of twilight purgatory
That I should not have said was merited.
I gave myself indeed a sprig of honor,
Or satisfaction, for the pride I found
In having redeemed myself from a taskmaster
Who only laughed at me and used his whip
When I defied him. Atlas called him paint;
I called him art; and Amaranth called him
    death—
Unless I fled from him and set my steps
Away from here for ever. If I'm here long,
I may go prowling down again alone
To those dim wharves where that unholy boat,
With Ipswich and his crew, all singing drunk,
Steamed off to sink; and then I may go farther—
If Amaranth will let me."

            "He will not,"
Said Evensong. "For recondite good reasons,
He means to keep you here for a long time—
I fear for always, though I mourn to say so.
There's talk abroad of Ipswich and his vessel,
And not much grief. There's no such playful
    way
Out of the past as theirs; and since they foun-
    dered
Shouting, with Ipswich's imperial drink
Warming and permeating their perceptions
With a wrong promise, we should be fools, or
    worse,

To wish them back. We don't know where they
    are."

"I was near saying that I know as well
Where they are as where I am," Fargo said,
And paused. There was a clear sound of a
    scratching
Outside the door; and Evensong said, "Ah,
My friend and fellow-lodger. By your leave,
I'll ask him to come in."

                "How do you do,"
Said Ampersand. With a superior tread
Of ease and ownership that made no noise,
He walked along to Fargo and jumped up
Softly into a chair not far from him,
And sat there like his name—with his tail round
    him
Like a black serpent. "I came in," said he,
"To see the picture."

           "If you came for that,"
Said Fargo, "there'll be one more disappoint-
    ment
For me to count in my long list of them
Since I came back. But I'm past all reproach,
Which has no current worth or meaning here.
I thought you might be coming to see me."

"Not so," said Ampersand, with a red yawn,
"I came to see the picture. Men go hungry,

And travel far, leaving their homes behind them
And their wives eating scraps, all to see pictures
That hungry men have painted. Art is cruel,
And so is nature; and if both are cruel,
What's left that isn't?"

        "I don't know," said Fargo;
"I'm hungry to find out. We'll talk about it.
Well, here is your new master, or new friend,
On canvas, and awaiting your opinion.
And what is your opinion?"

        "I don't like it,"
Said Ampersand—who promptly caught a fly
And anxiously chewed air until he found it.
"Excuse me. He was flying to his fate,
And here was I, ordained to swallow him.
You call it nature's law. I, being a cat,
Call it a problematical free will.
If there's a difference, no philosophers,
I'm told, have caught it yet. No, I don't like
    it—
I mean the picture. And if you have eyes
That are not liars, you are not proud of it
Along your back. There are no crinkles in it.
Why do you do it? You were here before,
I am informed; and why are you here now?
You must know where you are. Miss Watchman
    knew,
Although she never said it—not even to me.

And there was not much that I didn't know
About Miss Watchman. She told everything
To me—except that she knew where she was.
But she liked writing more than she liked truth,
Or life, and I'm not saying that she was foolish,
Or self-destroyed, in doing what she liked best.
When I can seize the possibility
Of doing what I like best, I always do it;
And I have no devouring aspirations
Consuming me with unacknowledged lies.
The more I learn of men's and women's folly
In trying to make their wishes their belief,
The more I'm rather content to be a cat;
And cats, you may have guessed, are not with-
    out
Their ingrained and especial vanities,
For which there is no cure. Nature in us
Is more intractable and peremptory;
Wherefore you call us feral and ferocious,
Which is unfair to us; for the same God
Who sees a sparrow on the ground shows us
The way to catch him, and we cannot choose.
You can, you say; and you have certainly
An instinct that appears more flexible
And less confined and less inexorable
Than ours. And if you have one, I mean really,
There should be freedom in you to explain
Why, for God's infinite sake, you are still paint-
    ing,
And why you have come back."

[86]

"If you are asking,
As well as Amaranth and Evensong,
And all their friends, I shall undoubtedly
Go down to those dim wharves and drown my-
     self,"
Said Fargo; "for I cannot answer you.
Almost I wish that Ipswich had prevailed
In luring me on board his hissing ship,
And blown me with it into the black water
That you will find down there."

            "I shall not find it,"
Said Ampersand. "You may have all the water
That I can't drink, which will be most of it.
Water was necessary, I was told,
To make me clean, but there was always blood
Before I would believe it."

            "So it is here
I find you, Fargo," Amaranth said, behind him.
"Well, you are safer here with Ampersand
And Evensong than with the grave-diggers.
And you are not so hostile, Ampersand,
As heretofore. Unless your face tells nothing,
You have been meditating and repenting."

"I have been ruminating and revolving
Ultimate thoughts, and had forgotten you,"
Said Ampersand. "If all had eyes like mine,
The darkness of our disappearances

Might have a transience and a diminution.
There's Atlas. Would you bring him back to
    us,
For rage and revelation to slay twice?
Since Evensong has given me a new home,
And all is changed, I'm full of afterthoughts
And inferences. Have you seen Fargo's picture?"

"I see it," said Amaranth; and Lawyer Figg,
Appearing imperceptibly, said "Yes,
I'm seeing it now."—"And I," said Doctor
    Styx.—
"And I," said Flax.

        "You are all seeing it,"
Said Fargo; "and so far as I'm the martyr,
There's no more to be said. I have no thirst
For praise that is not coming—and if it came,
Would only be salt water for the shipwrecked.
Your faces are your news; and I have read it
In headlines heavier than your reticence
Before you came. I ask with Ampersand,
And with you all together, why am I here?
It is my turn to ask."

        "We are all here,"
Said Amaranth, "to pay a pilgrimage—
The least we owe—to Atlas, who is now
The profanation of the grave-diggers.
Before oblivion blots and mingles it

[88]

With dreams of kings and slaves who are for-
    gotten,
His reckoning of an increment not there
Merits a breath of our commemoration.
I shall go charitably to the grave
Of one for whom ambition was a monster."

"And I," said Evensong. "Incidentally,
I have composed for him an elegy
Of sorts, and will play there, if you are patient,
The burden of it. Atlas will not mind.
It will not ruin us to remember him
And his discrepancies for a few minutes.
Always excepting Amaranth, who murmurs,
Forgive me if I see not one of us
So bent with eminence that he cannot walk,
And cannot spare a twinge of it for Atlas.
I shall go meekly to the funeral
Of one whose exultation so betrayed
And wasted him."

            "And so shall I," said Fargo;
"And I shall go with no commiseration
Of one whose way from here, if I stay here,
May still be mine."—"And I," said Lawyer
    Figg.—
"And I," said Doctor Styx.—"And I," said
    Flax.—
"I also; I like funerals, and promote
    Mortality myself—as when, perchance,

And on occasion, an elected mouse
And my compulsive predatory instinct
Combine and synchronize with my desire,"
Said Ampersand.—So there was Amaranth,
The Reverend Pascal Flax, and Doctor Styx,
And there was Lawyer Figg, and there was
    Fargo,
And there was Evensong, and Ampersand,
All going to the funeral. Evensong,
Descending, led the way; and after them,
The picture now forgotten, Fargo followed.

Now there were graves again surrounding him,
And everywhere as far ahead of him
As vision followed sight. He saw them now
Like waves, interminably motionless
And held by some unnatural command
In solid calm upon a sea of earth,
Where there was never to be storm or change,
Or a sun shining. Fargo moved alone,
Painting himself in hues of a new fancy
As the last man alive, and without fear.
He knew that where there were so many
    graves
To see, in that same light that was not light,
If he walked on, and on, and far enough,
There must be one somewhere that had been
    waiting
Too long. If it was here that he must live
Till death remembered him and set him free,

There was no more to ask of Amaranth,
Or time, than to forget. But where he was
There was no time. And where was Amaranth,
And all the rest who had gone out with him
From that old room?

     Yes, here was Amaranth,
And here was Evensong, and all of them;
And on the ground, like things that had emerged
Unwillingly from where they lived in it,
Munching unsightly food, and tearing it
With earthy fingers, were the grave-diggers.
The foulest of them Fargo recognized
As the malignant one that first had hailed
And seized him in the street; and now he heard
  him
Laughing uncleanly and with ribald scorn
To his foul neighbors: "Fargo has come back.
He knew enough to run away from us,
But not enough to stay. We'll have him yet!
We'll throw him down alive into a hole
Deeper than this one we have made for Atlas.
We'll have him yet. Only a fool comes back
Who has been here, and gone. We'll have him
  yet!"

"Be still, and eat—you necessary vermin,"
Said Amaranth. "There's work still waiting for
  you,
And then your pay. There's pay for everything;
[91]

And your existence is a part of it—
For you, and for all near you."

                              "If you died
Without us, we should hear bells ringing for
    us,"
Said one; "and we should then have better names.
We know the dirt that's on us, and we like it."

"You do not know it yet," said Amaranth,
"And that is why you like it. Now be quiet
Until this man is buried, and then be gone.
If you were clean, you would be miserable;
Which is too much for you to comprehend
Till you are born again—if ever you are."—
"Yah, yah," said one of them; and they were
    quiet.

Before there was a last pounding of earth
On Atlas, Evensong played his elegy
With earnest execution to an end
That was a rueful silence, and then sighed.
"It is not seizing, it is not celestial,"
He said, "but once it would have shaken me
All up and down myself with ecstasy,
And prayerful thankfulness to the Almighty,
That Evensong should do it. But Amaranth,
With his remorseless if unwilling habit
Of showing us, if we let him, where we are,
Laid ecstasy and thankfulness together

With me in the same grave where days are
        buried;
And when he found that I was here securely,
Without incentive and without invention,
Too dream-worn and indifferent to escape,
He gave me resignation or destruction
As a cold choice. Slower than Pink and Atlas
In my pursuit of the omnivorous Why,
I am still here, and in a manner tuneful.
But I am not deceived. I wish to heaven
I were, but Amaranth would not have it so."

"You would not have it so," said Amaranth.
"I murmur in men's ears invisibly
My warning, and I wait—mostly in vain;
And even with you that are aware of me,
I do not hold a mirror to your faces
To make you see, or die."

                              "Or both, maybe,"
Said Lawyer Figg. He gazed in retrospect
Where the grave-diggers, who had done their
        work
With chuckling curses and insinuations,
Had left a mound on what had once been Atlas:
"There was a time when for a few first years
I could have seen myself as Atlas is,
And wished indeed that I saw more than fancy.
But that was not my way; and I doubt yet
If Pink and Atlas have achieved release—

Though I am not an artist or a poet,
And I have not yet ridden a blue horse
Beyond my observation over the hill.
If I'm a sorry lawyer, that's because
I should have been seized early and submerged
In forethought chilly enough to make me shiver
And think. I was too docile and too warm.
I followed others, and you see me now;
I followed them because I saw them shining;
And without asking whether or not the fuel
In me was one to make their sort of fire
And light, I came to learn that it was not.
There was a proper flame that all the while
Was burning in me, but I stifled it
Slowly with indolence and indecision.
One day I fanned it with a breath of hope,
And found that it was out. Since then, and now,
My knees and sleeves are all of me that shines.
But they are mine, and I have no reproach,
Or verdict, or vain censure for this man,
And none for Pink. I have not lived their lives.
I have not shared their pangs or felt their ter-
    rors
On their awakening here in the wrong world
That unassayed ambition said was right.
My only contribution at this hour
Is my suspicion that a mortal haste
Like theirs may not have hurried them on so far
As they foresaw. I do not see them here,
And cannot follow them to tell you more.

AMARANTH

I am not mystical. But there's a jarring
Somewhere in this for me, and for the most
Of mankind, I believe; and I suspect
Without it there would not be trees enough
To make the paper that would hold the news
Of those who might no longer stay with us."

"Our friend and eminent horse-leech, Doctor
        Styx,
Owes you his next imperative attention,"
Said Evensong: "Your jam has all gone sour,
And you have covered your bad bread with it
Too heavily. The unlovely sight of Atlas,
Before we buried him, has turned everything;
But it will fade, as we shall."

                        Doctor Styx,
After the time of an inquiring glance
At Amaranth, who said nothing, looked at Figg
To reprimand him with a stern grimace:
"My bilious and invincible torch-bearer,
Listen to Evensong. Attend him shrewdly,
And you'll see shadows that are not so black
For some of us. If you must have black things
To see, why not see Ampersand, who sits
Ungrieved and with a firmness on the grave
That we have made for Atlas? There's a lesson
In him, and for us all, of independence,
If there's not one of courtesy. He's not saying
That all cats who have no-one to call Father

Should therefor curse their birth and drown
    themselves.
He looks away where there are distances
That are unknown and unimaginable,
And maybe for the reason of their dimness
Are more profound for him in their perspec-
    tive
Than Atlas, in the ground there, is for me.
He looks to me as if he had forgotten
All about Atlas; and he may have learned
In Egypt, where his import and importance
Were stated and established, that his rights
Are to sit where he will, if not removed,
And see what things he may. I cannot see them
With your eyes, Figg, more than I can with his;
And on the whole, if mine were to be lost,
I'd rather see them with his eyes than yours.
Things I can see with mine I know are there,
And should have known their purpose long ago.
If I had known them where they waited then,
My hands and faculties would be grateful now
For grasping them. Pink, in his diagnosis
Of my complaint, was nearer the physician
Than I was; and his candle might have burned
Longer, and with a wider light around it,
If Amaranth had waylaid him in his youth,
And held him and compelled him till he saw.
Figg feeds himself with mystery that he feels,
And cannot name. No man that I have met
Has ever named it with a word that tells me

More than a clock says. As for seeking it,
Or flying from here in a malignant rage
Of disillusionment—well, I suspect
I'm too indifferent, or we'll say too lazy.
Say what you will; I shall not writhe, or suffer.
I'm so inured to uselessness, maybe,
That moral torture and eternal doubt
That others feel leave me uninterested.
Let a man come to me with a disease
That I've a name for, I'll try not to kill him;
But let another man say the man's alive
When he is dead, I shall know what to call
    him."

"You mean," said Evensong, "if indirectly,
That you believe yourself, and all who live,
To be in essence, and in everything,
Identical in revealed futility
With what we buried when we buried Atlas.
The rest, you say, is nothing. Some would say
The rest is Atlas."

           "And I have to say it,"
Said Flax, the clergyman. "But if you pursue me
For more than I may tell, I shall be silent.
In the forgotten graveyard of the gods
There are so many that have come and gone
That I am lost among them. Most of them
Had better be called dead than their inventors—
Who must once have had life to fashion them,

As Pink said, of their fears. There is no God
For me to fear, or none that I may find,
Or feel, except a living one within me,
Who tells me clearly, when I question him,
That he is there. There is no name for him,
For names are only words. There was a time
When I thought words were life. There was a
    time
When I might have calumniated Atlas,
Branding him as a culprit and a sinner
To let himself be crushed under the weight
Of his house falling round him. But the God
That is within me tells me now that Atlas
Lived in another house that was not mine,
And that I am not told what might have hap-
    pened
If my house had been his. We are too brisk
In our assumption of another's lightness
Under a burden we have never felt,
And too remiss in calling ourselves liars
For saying so well so much more than we know.
Theology fell to pieces on my pulpit
Before I learned that I was telling lies
To friends who knew it. But my God was left
Within me—to be stirred there more by sloth,
Perhaps, than by revealed iniquity.
So, friends, I cannot answer you for Atlas.
All I can tell you is, that when I found
My house was falling, I fled out of it;
And that if I should fail to fly again,

The God within me would be felt and heard—
Although it might be quiet if it was there
Alone with only pain waiting for death.
I leave you to your several estimations
Of what I mean. We shall be here once more
Together, nor long from now, with Pink to
    bring us;
And I shall tell you only the same story—
Or better, none—when we are done with him.
There are complexities and reservations
Where there are poets, for they are alone,
Wherever they are. They are like Amper-
    sand;
They do not like us if we harass them
Unseasonably. I think it would be safer,
And more for our well-being and for our peace,
If we should let him hang for a while longer.
Our visitation, coming unforeseen
And unsolicited a second time,
Might only vex him. Though he fail, or die,
The poet somehow has the best of us;
He has a gauge for us that we have not."

"Pink had a gauge for me," said Doctor Styx;
"I could see that, but not his reading of it,
    For I'm an indifferent reader in the dark.
'I am as dead as I shall ever be,'
    He said; and that's what men who hang them-
        selves
    Do not say generally to a physician.

If I can't tell you whether a man's alive
Or not alive, don't ask me why I'm here,
Or why I should be anywhere. I don't know."

"And he had one for me," said Evensong;
"And while I mean to mourn apropriately,
  And for some time, his going away from us,
  I shall endure devotedly the scission
  And rift, I think."

                    "You are not thinking now,"
Said Amaranth; "you are struggling not to
    think.
The stings he left in you would not be itching
Without the lingering acid of some truth.
When Pink is here, you may be here some-
    times,
To ponder on his end and to ask whether
Or not it is the end. Your friend the doctor,
Whenever he says to you that Pink is dead,
Will tell you that it is. Your friend the preacher,
So far as words are his interpreters,
Weighs evil in more discriminating scales
Then heretofore, and says he cannot say
For certain what is evil. Your friend the lawyer,
Not yet assured of his illumination,
Would rather conserve the glimmer he thinks
    he has
Than blow it out. I hope you may all live
Until you are all sure you are not sorry,

Even here in the wrong world, that you were
    born.
And you, Styx, have a reason to live longer,
For you have more to learn. If I should an-
    swer
Your last unhappy question, you would still
Be asking; for the words that you may hear
Are like small shot that fly with a large noise
To shatter stars and bring them down to you
In dust for you to study. And if you had it,
You would have dust like this you cannot read
Where you are now. Fargo, the time has come
For you to tell me that my eyes have in them
Nothing for you to fear; for now you know
That once having heard my voice and heeded it,
Henceforth you are the stronger of the two.
Now it is clear that you have come to us
Unwillingly, and by no command of mine,
To see, and to be sure. When you are gone
From us, and are a memory here behind you,
We shall all know that you are coming back
To this place again never. So remember
A little, once in a while, of what it was
That you were leaving when you went from
    here.
If you are looking down now to find Atlas,
He is not there. You don't know where he is,
Fargo; and there is more doubt haunting you
Than sorrow. Never be sorry for the dead—
Lament them as you may, or treasure them;

And never build a stairway for a swallow."
Reluctantly, and with a premonition
Of change without a name compelling him,
Fargo, employed with his unanswered thoughts
Of Atlas, raised his eyes and found himself
Alone with Amaranth and Evensong.
Figg, Styx, and Flax, and Ampersand had van-
    ished,
And there were no more graves. He looked
    again,
And even the grave of Atlas was not there.
Mist, like a moving carpet on the ground,
Was over everything; and through the sky,
That for so long had been a veil of gray,
There was a coming of another color.

Amaranth said, "My eyes have nothing in them,
For you, that you may not see now with yours.
They did not summon you, but it is well
For you that you came back. Now you are sure,
And you are free. I cannot hold you here."

"Farewell," said Evensong. "If I had known,
I should have made a music of departure
That might have followed you for a short way.
Its eminent element would not have pierced
Or thrilled or melted you especially,
Though I should have enjoyed inditing it,
And with no injury to muse or man.
Farewell, and may your pumps unceasingly

Pour strength and blessing on you, and no paint.
Think of me as one fixed here in this place
Because he saw too late to go away.
Think of me as a friend who is remote,
Yet real as islands that you cannot see."

"Farewell," said Amaranth. "Remember me
As one who may not measure what he does,
More than fate may. If it were possible,
I should hold only pleasure in my eyes
For those who see too late. You heard my voice,
And heeded it, not knowing whose voice it was.
Many have heard it, and have only covered
Their fears and indecisions and misgivings
More resolutely with their vanities;
And under such an unsubstantial armor
Against the slow rust of discovery,
Must choose rather to strive and starve and
        fail,
And be forgotten, than to feel their names
In my pursuing murmur—which is mine
Because a mightier voice than you have heard
Is over mine the master. To a few
I murmur not in vain: they fly from here
As you did, and I see no more of them
Where, far from this miasma of delusion
They know the best there is for man to know;
They know the peace of reason. To a few
I show myself; but only the resigned
And reconciled will own me as a friend.

[103]

And all this you have seen. You are not here
To stay with us; and you are wiser now
For your return. You will not come again.
Remember me . . . The name was Ama-
        ranth . . .
The flower . . . that never . . . fades . . ."

                    "But you are fading!"
Said Fargo. "You and Evensong are fading.
Where are you going? And where has all this
        light
Come from so suddenly? Both of you are fad-
        ing—
Into a mist—a white mist. You are crumbling.
Your faces!—they are going."

                    While he spoke,
The world around him flamed amazingly
With light that comforted and startled him
With joy, and with ineffable release.
There was a picture of unrolling moments
In a full morning light, and out of it
Familiar walls and windows were emerging
From an inscrutable white mist that melted
Transparently to air; and there were fading
Two shapes that had no longer any form.
Fargo, partly awake, with eyes half open,
Saw sunlight and deliverance, and all through
        him
Felt a slow gratitude that he was hearing

Outside, somewhere, at last, the sound of liv-
    ing—
Mixed with a quaint regret that he was seeing
The last of Amaranth and Evensong.